W9-DEI-279

There is a $1.00 fine for removing bar code labels

NorthWest Arkansas Community College
Learning Resource Center

TIPS FROM THE TOUR

Edited by Peter McCleery
Associate Editor, Golf Digest

With Applications For Your Game
by Chuck Cook

Illustrated by Jim McQueen and Elmer Wexler

A Golf Digest Book

Published by Golf Digest/Tennis, Inc.
A New York Times Company
5520 Park Avenue
Box 395
Trumbull, Connecticut 06611-0395

Trade book distribution by
Simon and Schuster
A division of Simon & Schuster, Inc.
Simon & Schuster Building
Rockefeller Center
1230 Avenue of the Americas
New York, New York 10020

First printing, 1986
Manufactured in the
United States of America
Cover and book design by Nick DiDio
Printing and binding by R. R. Donnelley

Library of Congress Cataloging-in-Publication Data

Tips from the tour.

    "A Golf Digest book"—Spine.
    1. Golf. I. McCleery, Peter.
GV965.T54 1986   796.352   85-72332
ISBN 0-914178-77-6

CONTENTS

Foreword 4
How To Use This Book 6

I. FULL SWING 7
Fuzzy Zoeller 8
Miller Barber 12
Larry Nelson 16
Joey Sindelar 20
Payne Stewart 24
Tom Purtzer 28
Scott Hoch 32
Calvin Peete 36
Danny Edwards 40
Mike Sullivan 44
Jim Thorpe 48

II. SHORT GAME/SAND 53
Tom Kite 54
Lee Trevino 58
Mark Lye 62
Curtis Strange 66
Larry Mize 70
Wayne Levi 74

III. PUTTING 79
Bruce Lietzke 80
Patty Sheehan 84
D.A. Weibring 88
Hollis Stacy 92

IV. STRATEGY/MENTAL 97
Lanny Wadkins 98
John Mahaffey and JoAnne Carner 102
Corey Pavin 106
Brad Faxon 110
Roger Maltbie 114
Fred Couples with Jan Stephenson 118
David Edwards 122

V. SPECIALTY 127
Keith Fergus 128
Gary Koch 132
Gil Morgan 136
Chip Beck 140
Jay Haas 144
John Fought 148
Dave Eichelberger 152
Gardner Dickinson 156

FOREWORD

The original concept for the instruction series "Tips from the Tour" came from, of all people, PGA Tour Commissioner Deane Beman. Invited to a special meeting with the GOLF DIGEST editors in 1981, Beman was asked what new areas of golf instruction he thought we might cover. The commissioner, always a thoughtful student of the swing, suggested that we were overlooking an opportunity for our player-reader. While the magazine had featured bylined instruction articles from top players and teachers since its inception, Beman wondered out loud if we weren't neglecting many of the fresh young faces on the tour whose instruction brains hadn't been picked.

Out of that discussion blossomed monthly "Tips from the Tour," premiering in the July 1982 issue. When we first began presenting the tips, they were often labeled "for better players." The thinking was that many of the tour pros' ideas would be best suited to the more skilled amateur players—and anyway, even the less advanced players would want to read them, because all golfers have delusions of grandeur.

As time went by, we split the tips into two categories. One was still labeled "for better players" and featured the pros' swing theories and specialty shots. The other was called simply "Tips from the Tour," and was written by the defending champion of an upcoming tournament, recalling the instruction keys he or she used to win that particular event the previous year.

The tips presented in this collection are a combination of those two efforts written by 38 leading men, women and senior pros (two of the tips have co-authors). Among them, they have won an astounding 285 tournaments (including 33 major championships) and more than $48 million in prize money—and counting.

When it came time to package the tips in book form, however, it was felt we needed something to bring into focus for nontour players the various approaches advocated by the pros. Just rerunning the tips as they appeared in the magazine would be redundant. We decided we needed a respected teaching professional to bring a unifying voice to this collection, to clarify and amplify the instruction so that golfers at all skill levels could apply these stroke and strategy keys to their own games.

To that end we selected a man who is eminently qualified for the task. Chuck Cook, 41, a former instructor in the Golf Digest Schools, is now the director of the Academy of Golf at the Hills of Lakeway resort in Austin, Tex. His students range from tour stars like Tom Kite, Dave Stockton and Donna Caponi to high-handicap amateurs. He started in the Golf Digest program in 1977 as a range assistant ("I teed up balls for the other teachers because I wanted to listen to the lessons," he says) and proved to be such a quick learner that within two years he became a full-time instructor. Through that association, he worked with such renowned teachers as Bob Toski, Jim Flick, Peter Kostis and Davis Love. Subsequent assignments have paired him with such other outstanding instructors as John Jacobs, Phil Rodgers and Harvey Penick, a legend-in-residence at the nearby Austin Country Club. Cook was recently named the South Texas PGA's Harvey Penick "Teacher of the Year."

"Because of the people I've had the good fortune to work with, I have a lot of different ways I can teach," says Cook. "I can use Mr. Penick's ways or I can use Bob Toski's cues, depending on the student. I like to think there are many different ways to play this game—not just one way—and all those ways are represented in these tips. Everybody is different physically and mentally but everybody has to have a system to play with. The tour pros already have that. My job working with amateur players is to pick out which system works best for each particular person."

In his supplements to the 36 tips, Cook offers drills, mental images and underscores the key points to help you incorporate the tips into your shotmaking repertoire. It makes for a dynamic one-two-instruction punch. I'd like to thank Chuck for his illuminating insights, the tour pros who shared their thoughts with our editors in the field, and the commissioner, whose suggestion unwittingly spawned the idea in that meeting five years ago.

—Peter McCleery
Trumbull, Conn.
June 1986

HOW TO USE THIS BOOK

This book is a treasure trove of 36 tips from the pro tours, which have become a favorite feature in GOLF DIGEST since the series began in 1982. We have all wondered from time to time what the best players in the world are thinking about just before they hit a shot to win a tournament, or as they apply strategy for special situations and pull off some magical trick to escape from seemingly inescapable trouble. This book lets us in on that process. It is a rare look inside the thinking world of professional golf.

It is also a rare opportunity for amateur golfers—from advanced players down to beginners—to learn from the best by understanding how to apply these tips to their own games. First we must understand that every player on tour has developed the fundamentals necessary to good golf. They have a "system" for playing the game. Some of the tips represent special attention given to a part of their system that might have fallen into disrepair and undermined that fundamental system. Some are recent additions to the player's shot-making inventory, enhancing the system and the level at which he or she plays. In both instances, they are not meant to be a "cure-all" or replacement for sound fundamentals. Some of the tips might not even be compatible with your system of play. I am confident, however, that certain tips can have the same effect on your game as they did for, say, Calvin Peete or Curtis Strange. And so we've followed each tip with suggestions for your implementation plan—and its application to your level of play.

I hope you'll enjoy this collection for what it represents—a look at the thoughts and feelings of the world's greatest golfers and some recommendations that I think can help you to play just a little bit more like they do.

Chuck Cook
Austin, Tex.
May 1986

I

FULL
SWING

FULL SWING

Jim McQueen

Pull down the heel of the driver first on downswing

By FUZZY ZOELLER

They say you drive for show and putt for dough, but that's not always the case. It was my improved driving that put me in position to win the 1983 Sea Pines Heritage Classic; it's a tough course and if you're driving in the rough all the time, it's difficult to post a decent score.

Everybody has different gimmicks. We play so much golf out here that you have to have something to remind you to do certain things in your swing. With the driver, I have a habit of sliding the club out so that the ball is lined up facing the heel or hosel instead of the screws or the sweet spot. This tells me to try to pull the heel of the clubhead down first in my downswing.

Most amateurs take the club back OK, but when they get to the top they throw it down instead of swinging it. With that little sliding motion out to the heel I get away from that swinging-over-the-top motion. Ken Venturi once said on TV that this makes me bring the club a little more inside, but it really doesn't. It's just a mental reminder that works for me and might do the same for you.

Winner of nine tournaments and more than $1.8 million in 11 years on the PGA Tour, Zoeller's victories include the 1979 Masters, 1984 U.S. Open and at press time, the Heritage Classic for the second time in four years. He recovered from major back surgery in 1985 to win the Hertz Bay Hill Classic and $244,003 for the year.

FULL SWING

Swing a bottle filled with water and don't get wet

The method Fuzzy uses to eliminate the throwing or "casting" of the club is a little unorthodox but it obviously works for him. As a word of warning, the excess bending over at address and straightening through impact is hard on the back and I would not recommend it to anyone with back problems. However, if your problem is casting the club from the top, I'd certainly recommend that you try it.

One of the best devices I know of to create the proper "feel" of swinging a club is to get an empty 2-liter soda bottle and put a couple of inches of water in the bottom of it. With the cap off, hold the neck of the bottle and practice swinging the bottle back and through without spilling any water. If you are swinging correctly, you'll stay nice and dry, but if you try to throw it from the top, you'll get a wet reminder of what you're doing wrong. This will help eliminate any tendency to "throw away" the centrifugal force necessary for good clubhead speed.

FULL SWING

For smooth tempo, start your swing low and slow

By MILLER BARBER

What stands out most in my mind in winning three Senior Open championships is my good tempo. When I'm in a good groove, the pace of my swing is smooth and slow all week. Like most golfers, I have a tendency to speed up. As a result I don't make solid contact with the ball when I'm swinging fast. But in winning the Senior Open titles in Portland in '82, Rochester, N.Y., in '84 and Lake Tahoe, Nev., in 1985, I just tried to keep my tempo under control, and it worked.

My swing thought is to start the club *low and slow* away from the ball for the first six or eight inches. I figure if you're slow at the start, you'll be slow throughout the swing. If you start fast, you're a goner. Fast has never won anything except on a racetrack. Even now, when I start mis-hitting shots I concentrate on how the club moves away from the ball for the first six or eight inches. Don't be in a hurry. You can never swing too slowly as far as I'm concerned; your natural reflexes won't allow that. Just think of those critical inches at the start of your swing and begin the takeaway low and slow.

Barber has won 18 tournaments in five years on the Senior PGA Tour, including the 1982, 1984 and 1985 U.S. Senior Open. From 1967 through 1974, he won at least one tournament a year on the PGA Tour, a feat matched only by Jack Nicklaus.

Vary your swing speeds to find your "best beat"

Swinging with the correct tempo is an important fundamental of good golf. However, not all players have the same tempo at which they perform best. But all players have their best "beat." For instance, Tom Watson and Lanny Wadkins have a faster beat to their swings than, say, Ben Crenshaw or Sam Snead. Imagine trying to get Snead to swing at the same pace as Watson, or Wadkins to swing at the same beat as Crenshaw. What all four players have done is what Miller Barber did at the Senior Open. He discovered his best beat.

To find your best beat, I recommend the "Goldilocks" drill. Hit some shots (chips or pitches are OK) using your normal beat, then increase the pace of your swing for a while. After doing this, change gears and hit some shots at a slower pace than normal. By varying the beat, you will find out which one is most comfortable for you. Or as Goldilocks says, "Just right."

FULL SWING

Follow the pane to swing on plane

By LARRY NELSON

On the takeaway, I like to feel that the club is traveling straight back from the ball and right up the plane. Envisioning it moving along a pane of glass helps. This counteracts a tendency many good players have to yank the club inside too quickly with the hands on the takeaway, which causes them to lock up at the top of the backswing and come over the ball starting down.

Eventually, the club has to move to the inside, of course, but getting it started back correctly adds to your extension and gives you a bigger swing arc. It lets you get behind the ball better on the backswing, with your shoulders turning rather than tilting. This keeps the club on a better plane back and through the swing. Practicing this will help you hit the ball farther and straighter, as it does me.

Winner of seven tournaments and more than $1.5 million in 12 years on the PGA Tour, including 1981 PGA Championship and 1983 U.S. Open, Nelson starred on the U.S. Ryder Cup team in 1979 and 1981 and was named Golf Digest's Most Improved Male Professional in 1979, when he won two tournaments and finished second on the money list with $281,022.

To catch your right plane, try the "belly button drill"

If you notice the pane of glass over Larry's shoulder, you'll see that the club can be "on plane" anywhere on that pane. Therefore, before the club can come inside, it must come *up* an equal amount. Keeping the club low and taking it inside will take it off plane, and picking the club up to the outside also goes off plane. Blending the up with the inside is the key.

A good way to do this is to initiate your backswing with your turn, keeping your arms and club in the same relationship with your body as they were at address. Using a clock image, if the ball is at 6 o'clock in your stance the "one-piece takeaway" of body, arms and club should remain connected to about 8:30. From there, the arms and wrists can swing from the turn and carry the club back the rest of the way.

A drill that will help you achieve this is one I call the "belly button drill." Take a club and stick the butt end of it into your belly button. Then slide your hands down the shaft and grip the club with your normal extension. Your hands will now be on the steel. From there bend over to your normal posture. Practice turning your belly button while just holding the butt end of the club against your middle and you'll feel the natural in-and-up arc the club should take.

FULL SWING

Make a full turn for full control

By JOEY SINDELAR

Under pressure, do you switch to a three-quarter swing for greater control? I'd recommend just the opposite. For complete control, make a full shoulder turn, as big as you possibly can, the way the great players like Tom Watson and Jack Nicklaus do.

That full turn allows the various parts of your body to work in proper sequence on the downswing (see illustration). If you cut the turn short, some parts have to work extra hard and extra fast, and that leads to mis-hits. When I shorten my turn I tend to try to hit the ball harder with my hands. The full turn gives my hands time to work naturally, so I don't have to over-work them.

A full turn will help maintain your accuracy—and increase your power.

Sindelar won $282,762 in 1985, his second year on the PGA Tour, including victories in the Greater Greensboro Open and B.C. Open. A three-time All-American at Ohio State, he won 10 collegiate titles, including the 1981 Big Ten championship by 12 strokes.

Think of a swinging door opening and closing to feel a good turn

A good turn (along with a good grip) is the hallmark of most good players. Your body should work like a swinging door. On the back-swing, your body opens. On the downswing, your body closes (square like a door) and on the follow-through, the body opens

again. To create the correct path, the turn should be balanced; that is, a 90 degree turn to the right should be balanced with a 90 degree turn to the left.

In the illustration of Joey Sindelar, I noticed he's made a good turn of the shoulders but not much with his hips. If you are older, thick-waisted or less flexible, you might want to allow your hips to turn more than this strong and supple tour pro does.

To get the feeling of a good turn, use the "belly button drill" described in the previous tip (Larry Nelson) but don't bend over—stand straight up. Turn to the right until your club shaft is parallel to the target line, then turn to the left until the shaft is again parallel to the target line. You'll feel and see the natural opening and closing of the door to better golf.

FULL SWING

Narrow your stance for better tempo, turn

By PAYNE STEWART

The week before the 1983 Walt Disney World Classic, I was doing an outing in Jamaica, and it seemed a good time to work on my swing. Two problems had crept up on me: my stance had become too wide with the driver and my swing tempo was too fast.

I think the ideal stance width is narrower than most average players think. If you get your feet too wide at address, it restricts your turn during the swing. The outsides of your golf shoes should be about even with the outsides of your shoulders. That was easy for me to correct.

Good tempo took a little more work. I tried to slow down my swing on the practice tee by hitting shots less than my full distance. For example, I hit my normal 4-iron 190 yards. But I practiced making a full swing and hitting the 4-iron only 150. Then gradually I increased the distance—150, 160, 170, 180—up to my normal level. I still was swinging easily, but going at it just a little harder at the bottom. I left Jamaica feeling so good I couldn't wait to get to Orlando.

In the second round at Disney World, I hit 18 greens in regulation and shot 64. It was the first time I'd ever putted for 18 birdies in a round. My confidence kept building and I won by two strokes. Good tempo tends to carry you like that.

Stewart has won the 1982 Quad Cities Open, the 1983 Walt Disney World Classic and $805,420 in five years on the PGA Tour. Known for his colorful plus fours, Stewart ranked No. 1 on the tour in 1985 in a composite of the nine statistical categories and finished one stroke behind winner Sandy Lyle in the 1985 British Open.

FULL SWING

Check the width of your stance against a post or clubshaft

The width of your stance is a critical factor in your swing. It is the "bridge" which allows your weight to shift properly. Too narrow a stance and you can't get enough weight shift. Too wide a stance requires a swaying movement to create the shift. If your width is correct, you can turn all of your upper body behind the ball on the backswing and turn all of your upper-body weight past your ball position on the follow-through without swaying (moving your spine).

You can again use a shaft or post to help you find the width that will give you your best swing foundation. The shaft or post must be tall enough to reach your shoulder line;

put it in the ground where your ball position would be. With a good player, when he swings back with an iron his back remains on that post, but all of his weight is *behind* it. And when he follows through, his back is still on that post. If your width is too narrow, you will get a reverse shift with your weight in front of the ball on the backswing. If you are too wide, your back moves off the post as you sway to the right going back; then you have to sway again on the downswing to get back to your left side.

Another self-test: If your stance is the correct width, your knees will be able to touch on the follow-through.

Turn— don't slide— for consistency

By TOM PURTZER

Recently I fell into a bad habit common among a lot of players. I was sliding my hips in the swing instead of turning. The problem with sliding the hips to the right on the backswing is that you then have to slide them to the left on the forward swing. Unless they slide back the same distance, you'll be inconsistent.

To correct this, I learned a simple practice device. I have my caddie hold a club against my right hip. If I slide to the right the shaft moves. If I turn properly, the shaft remains motionless and my body remains in contact with the shaft throughout the swing.

Get a friend to help you the way my caddie did—and then do the same for him. To coin a phrase that's trite but true, one good "turn" deserves another.

Winner of $938,599 in 11 years on the PGA Tour, Purtzer's victories include the 1977 Glen Campbell-Los Angeles Open and the 1984 Phoenix Open in his hometown. One of the longest drivers on tour, he has averaged well over 270 yards in each of the last five seasons (1981-1985).

Create your own "swing barrel" and learn to turn inside it

In the proper swing, the body turns around the spine. The spine serves as the hinge to the swing. Excessive sliding of the hips will cause the bottom "hinge" to come loose, making the "door" (your swing) swing at a tilted angle. When this occurs, solid club-ball contact becomes a sometime thing at best and a "never happened" at worst.

To get the feeling of the correct turning of the hips, that venerable swing cue of "swing in a barrel" is especially apt. To create your own barrel, use two golf shafts and stick them in the ground next to your legs, slightly outside the width of your normal stance. What you want to do is make your backswing without sliding off the ball and coming into body contact with the shaft next to your right leg. Then complete your swing without sliding too far forward into the shaft on the left. Practice until you can swing "inside the barrel."

Left knee toward target to make ball go there, too

By SCOTT HOCH

My first move in the forward swing is to drive my left knee toward the target, keeping it going in that direction as long as I can throughout the shot without losing my balance.

This keeps my lower body from spinning out and keeps me from going over the top. If the left side goes left too quickly, the right side has to follow. This move drops my arms onto an inside path and helps me keep my right side under the left through impact. This results in more extension and acceleration, giving me more distance, not to mention accuracy.

You need to do this with every club, but the longer the club the more chance you have of spinning out, so the more you have to accentuate driving that left knee toward the target.

This thought is good for anybody, if it doesn't make you too leg conscious and adversely affect the swinging of your arms, but it's especially good for the better player who has the ability to time the swinging of his arms with his leg motion.

Winner of the 1980 and 1984 Quad Cities Open, Hoch has earned $844,037 in six seasons on the PGA Tour. An outstanding collegiate player at Wake Forest, he played with Curtis Strange and Jay Haas on the 1975 NCAA title team.

Activate your lower body with a drill as simple as 1-2-3

To paraphrase Sir Isaac Newton, action creates reaction, and nothing is truer in the golf swing. As noted teacher Phil Rodgers says, a good golf swing looks like a pendulum, with most of the action occurring down below while the upper torso is more or less stable. Bad swings, on the other hand, can look like a metronome with the upper body doing all the moving while the lower body serves as an anchor.

To get the lower body acting and reacting, try this "1-2-3" drill: Hit balls with a shaft lying between your feet. Make a forward press with your right knee moving in front of the shaft (1). During the backswing, let the left knee move behind the shaft (2) and on the follow-through, let the right knee move past the shaft (3). This drill is an effective way to get you stepping in the right direction.

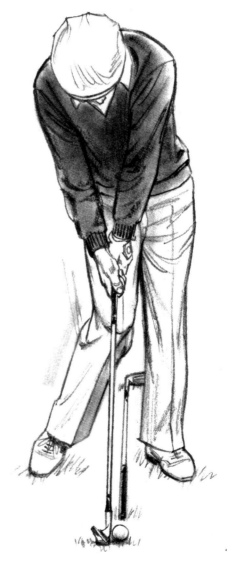

PEETE   -7
PATE   -5
COUPLES -5
IRWIN   -4

Jim McQuinn

For tempo and balance stay light on your feet

By CALVIN PEETE

Picking the decisive turning point in a tournament isn't always possible, but for me the key moment in the 1982 B.C. Open came on the 441-yard 13th when I holed a 2-iron from 204 yards. That came at a good time since I was in a tight race with Fuzzy Zoeller and Jerry Pate.

Obviously you can't practice holing 2-irons the way you practice bunker shots, but you can practice making smooth, balanced swings so that when you find yourself in a tight spot on the golf course, your swing will hold up.

Under pressure, my swing thoughts are "tempo and balance" and you can't have either if your weight isn't evenly distributed on both feet—not too much on either foot, nor toward your toes or heels. I think of my left foot as rolling to the right on the backswing. On the forward swing the left foot serves as an anchor and my right foot rolls toward the target as my weight shifts back to the left. I never consciously lift either heel off the ground.

I think of my feet as being similar to a governor on an engine. If I have good, light footwork I can't swing too fast when the heat is on—and if I swing too fast I can't have good footwork. Try my approach. You may not make a lot of eagles but you'll hit more fairways and greens—and take my word for it, that can pay off very nicely.

Winner of 12 tournaments in 10 years on the PGA Tour, including the 1985 Tournament Players Championhip and the 1986 USF&G Classic and Tournament of Champions. The straight-shooting Peete has led the tour in driving accuracy (hitting the fairway with his tee shots) for the past five years (1981-'85) and since 1982, has won more tournaments and more money than anyone else on tour.

Keep your knees close together by "staying under the shafts"

A good way to foster the footwork Calvin suggests is to reduce the gap between your knees. On the backswing, as your right hip turns off the target line your right leg will have a tendency to straighten slightly. Your left knee and leg will move toward this vacated spot, not toward the ball. On the follow-through the opposite will happen—your left hip clearing will straighten the left leg, and the right knee and leg will "fill the gap." The most talented ball-strikers finish their swings with their thighs actually touching.

To feel this motion, get two club-shafts and stick them in the ground across the top of your feet at address. As you swing, try to stay under the shafts. This makes your knees turn nicely and keeps your legs real close together, creating the rolling effect you're looking for.

FULL SWING

Jim McQueen

"Tie" your upper body to a post for better control

By DANNY EDWARDS

In any sport it's important to stay behind the object you're trying to propel forward, whether you're throwing it or striking it with something.

Even some better golfers I've seen often have too much movement in their upper bodies, especially as they start sliding toward the target on the forward swing. It's almost like trying to hit a moving target, because if there is movement up above, the ball is, in effect, moving in the opposite direction.

To combat this, I like to feel as if my upper body is tied to a post.

This thought keeps me from swaying both backward and forward. It makes me feel that my upper body is "tied together" and allows me to properly turn my shoulders under on the forward swing. It is especially effective for iron shots, because it helps get the ball higher so it lands softly on the green.

I don't recommend this thought to the higher handicapper because it could cause a reverse weight shift. But it's an excellent image for the better player who has already developed plenty of swing motion and now needs to learn how to control it.

In 11 years on the PGA Tour, Edwards has won $856,637 and five tournaments, including 1985 Pensacola Open. Older brother of touring pro David Edwards, he's also an avid race-car driver and collector.

Have a friend help you create a stable swing axis

As we mentioned in previous tips, there is a "post" in your swing, and that post is your spine. To understand the importance of a stable axis, imagine what would happen to a wheel on a car if the axle wasn't fixed. Just like that wheel, your swing would wobble in numerous directions. To relate this to clubhead speed, picture a roped tether ball attached to a post. As you swing the ball around the post, the greatest centrifugal force is generated. But if the post were allowed to move with the ball, the force would be greatly diminished.

To create the feel of a stable axis in your golf swing, have a steady-handed friend hold a club within four or five inches of either side of your head, to allow room for the head to rotate but not rock or move laterally. Hit practice balls while doing this and soon you'll have your upper body "posted" correctly.

FULL SWING

Knees are the key to a good pivot

By MIKE SULLIVAN

One crucial factor in the good player's swing is a good pivot. Too many golfers never get off their left sides during the swing. A good player, however, will make his weight go to the right on the backswing and return to the left on the forward swing. I find the best way to insure this is to think of the movement of the knees relative to my ball position in both directions.

On the backswing, turn the upper body and get the left knee behind the ball. Going forward, swing the arms and hands and get the right knee to the ball at the same time as the clubhead.

If you time these movements properly, you'll get the correct weight transfer. You'll get behind the ball on your backswing, and your legs will support your arm swing going forward. This will give you the leverage you need for longer and straighter shots.

Sullivan has won the 1980 Southern Open and $621,395 in nine years on the PGA Tour. He also won the unofficial 1984 Shootout at Jeremy Ranch on the Senior PGA Tour with Don January.

FULL SWING

Imagine turning against a wall to stop the "blocks"

The main reason most players fail to pivot correctly is because they are "blocked" out. In other words, before the left side can turn away from the ball on the backswing, the right side must get out of the way and likewise, before the right side can turn through the shot, the left side has to get out of the way.

To help you create the proper pivot, imagine a wall running up the length of your body 6 to 8 inches in front of you. Turn the right side off the wall on the backswing and then let the left side run along the wall. On the follow-through, turn the left side off the wall and let the right side run along it. If, for instance, the left side doesn't get out of the way, the right side will have nowhere to go but "over the top" of the wall.

FULL SWING

Choke up on the driver—don't give up

By JIM THORPE

On a tight driving hole where I definitely need to put the ball in the fairway, I hate to abandon my driver for a 3-wood because I lose distance that way. Especially on the long par 4s or the par 5s, I need all the distance I can get because I'm not the best iron player in the world.

So instead of giving up on the driver, I choke up on it. I grip it down about one to 1½ inches. That gives me more clubhead control but still allows me to take a good, firm swing. It also puts me down just a little closer to the ball, and this seems to help my balance.

When I'm driving the ball well, it gives me confidence in the rest of my game. If I have the confidence to use the driver even on tight holes, I feel I have control of the clubhead on all my shots. Try it.

Thorpe broke through in 1985 with his first tour victories, beating Jack Nicklaus at the Greater Milwaukee Open and Jack Renner in the final match at the Seiko-Tucson Match Play Championship. He lost a memorable playoff to amateur Scott Verplank in the 1985 Western Open, but still collected first-prize money of $90,000. He finished the year fourth on money list with $379,091 and was named Golf Digest's Most Improved Male Professional.

FULL SWING

Choking up makes it easier for clubhead to catch up with body, arms

There are several advantages to shortening up on your driver. First of all, history tells us that Byron Nelson and Jack Nicklaus, to name a couple of great players, both did it because their drivers were shorter than standard length. As you choke up on the driver, two good things happen. First, the shaft stiffens, creating less flutter in the clubhead and thus producing straighter shots. Second, timing becomes easier.

To understand this advantage, imagine a circular track with three lanes. The inside lane is occupied by the body turn and is a relatively short arc. The arms occupy the middle lane which is a longer arc than the body turn's. Finally, the clubhead arc represents the outside lane which is the longest.

In golf, all three start at the same place and must finish in a dead heat to hit a straight shot. Choking up on the driver reduces the length of that outside arc, thus requiring less clubhead speed to "catch up" with the other two racers (i.e., your body and arms) at the moment of truth—impact.

SHORT GAME/ SAND

SHORT GAME/SAND

Jim McQueen

Let hands work in "putting" chip

By TOM KITE

O n the 15th hole at Bay Hill, the first hole of my playoff with Jack Nicklaus and Denis Watson for the 1982 Bay Hill Classic title, my 8-iron second shot spun about three feet off the green onto the short fringe, 18 feet to the left of the hole.

I faced a shot that was slightly uphill with a right-to-left break, and I decided to chip it with an 8-iron. That way the ball wouldn't get caught up in the fringe and I'd have a better chance of getting it rolling on line. I was trying to make it, and I did, for the victory.

For chips like this, I try to set up as nearly as possible as I do for a putt. I use my putting grip, the reverse overlap, and stand fairly close to the ball with the club set slightly on the toe. I position the ball just slightly forward of the center of my stance and set my weight slightly on my left side to insure hitting down on the ball.

In putting, I use an arm-and-hand stroke, and I do the same thing for this type of chip shot. I keep the blade low, making a slow and rhythmic stroke as I do with my putter.

When I first started working with this shot I tried to take out the hands completely. I could hit the ball very straight but had no feel for distance. Now I make no effort to restrict the hand action and let it work in combination with the arms. I have much more control over distance without losing accuracy.

Winner of $2,525,327 and eight tournaments in 14 years on the PGA Tour. Kite was the tour's leading money winner in 1981 with $375,699 and has won more than $100,000 in each of the last 11 seasons. A two-time Vardon Trophy winner from Austin, Tex., Kite has worked extensively on his game with Harvey Penick and Chuck Cook, the co-author of this book.

For short-game skill, learn to let the clubhead pass your hands

There is a myth about the hands in the short game that may have hurt some players: that the hands have to stay in front of the clubhead at all times, never allowing the club to pass them. Actually, it's OK for the club to pass the hands. For a club to be swung in a true arc, the butt of the club should always point to the same place. This requires the low point of the arc to be underneath the spot where the butt of the club is pointing, after which the clubhead will begin to pass the hands. Notice the illustration of Tom (previous page) and you'll see this is true.

Here's a drill to get the feel of the clubhead passing. Set up in the position Tom suggests but use a 2-iron. Stand fairly close to the ball with the club set slightly on its toe, the ball just forward of center and your weight on your left side. But choke down until the butt of the club touches your stomach. Then make swings keeping the butt end touching you in the same place. While you won't be using any pronounced hand action, you'll still be able to feel the clubhead pass correctly.

The taller the grass, the tighter the grip

By LEE TREVINO

In the majors, the rough gets rougher. That was especially true in the PGA Championship at Shoal Creek in 1984 when the thick Bermuda grass made pitch and chip shots around the greens treacherous. Bluegrass is almost as bad.

But I have a rule for pitching and chipping out of tall grass that might make some of your shots from the rough easier: "The taller the grass, the tighter the grip."

If the rough is really tall and thick, I squeeze the club as tightly as I can. Why? So that I can keep it moving at a constant speed through the thick grass. And I want that speed to be the same speed on the downswing as it is on the backswing. I just start back gently and at the top I let it go, allowing my arms (with no wrist movement) to lead the clubhead through the ball.

If you grip the club too loosely on these pitches and chips, you're liable to catch the clubhead in the grass, slow it down and close the face. When you're trying to get the ball close, that can be deadly.

Trevino has won 27 tournaments and $3,177,975 in a rags-to-riches career on the PGA Tour. His victories include six major championships—his last one the 1984 PGA Championship at age 44. He burst on the scene in 1968 and won the U.S. Open. In 1971, he won the Open again, defeating Jack Nicklaus in a playoff at Merion and in a span of five weeks added the Canadian and British Open titles. Now a color analyst for NBC-TV's coverage of the PGA Tour, he's still a threat whenever he tees it up.

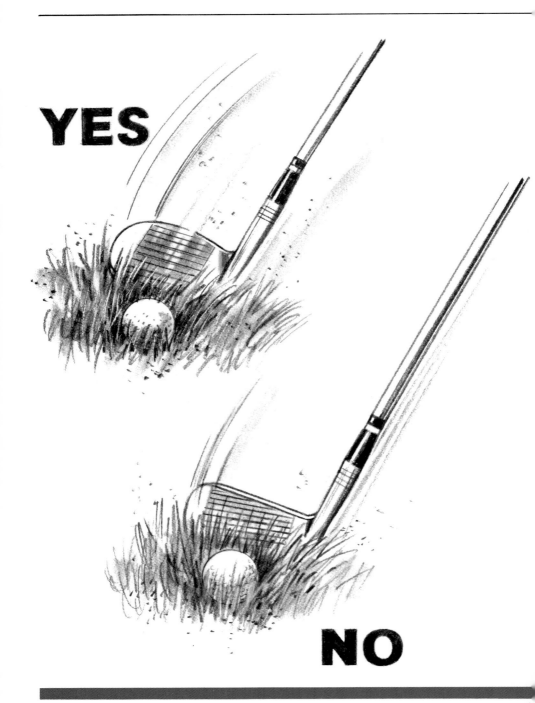

YES

NO

Be sure to use a sand wedge to get through that grass

The one suggestion I would add to Trevino's advice is to always use a sand wedge from high rough around the green. The reasons for this are several. First, the sand wedge has more loft than the other clubs, insuring that the ball will pop out of that tall grass. Secondly, the sand wedge is heavier, which helps the club get through the grass easier. Finally, the sand wedge has an angled flange, known as the "bounce" of the club. This bounce serves as a rudder to keep the club from digging in.

To hit high shots with the arms leading and a firm grip, be sure the clubface stays open so the club won't lose its loft. To hit lower shots in the same situation, put your weight left to produce a more up-and-down swing, thereby eliminating a lot of the grass between the club and the ball. In either case, make sure you've got the correct club, a sand wedge, in your hands to get the desired result.

Soften grip pressure for soft pitch

By MARK LYE

My pitch to the last green at the 1983 Bank of Boston Classic stands out in my mind as the most important shot of the tournament.

The 18th hole at Pleasant Valley is a par 5, but my second shot was long and finished 10 yards over the green, in high grass and in a slightly downhill lie. Not the best lie for the high, soft shot I needed to hit.

My one thought was to relax my hands and make a soft, smooth swing. The tendency when facing such a shot is to squeeze the grip for dear life, but that leads to tension and trouble.

By gripping lightly, you allow the weight and loft of the sand wedge to do the job, sliding through the grass and popping the ball out softly. It worked for me—the ball trickled down toward the hole, and I had my first tour win. I think it will work for you, too.

Winner of $769,421 in nine years on the PGA Tour, Lye won the 1983 Bank of Boston Classic by coming from eight shots behind on the last day to shoot 64 and win by a single shot over John Mahaffey, Jim Thorpe and Sammy Rachels. He finished the round birdie, par, birdie, birdie.

To produce softness under pressure, work on positions that require it

We would all like to be able to swing softly under pressure. Unfortunately, it doesn't always happen. Unless you play under pressure a lot, like the tour pros, it's sometimes hard to achieve. Peter Kostis, a top Golf Digest Schools instructor, once told me a good way to encourage it is to try to produce *positions* that *require* softness to reach them. For example, hitting a soft shot and finishing with both elbows flexed would require a loosening of the arms at address to achieve that flexing at the finish. Or making the clubhead finish close to your left ear would require soft hands to position it there. When my students are trying to hit a real soft shot, I've sometimes taken a magic marker and drawn a smiling face on the clubhead, then told them to follow through so that the smiling face on the clubhead looks at them. This requires a relaxed left wrist.

Again, if you play under pressure fairly frequently, you can think soft and it will happen. But for most of us, soft has to be "positioned." In other words, you have to work at it.

Cock club open for high, soft bunker shot

By CURTIS STRANGE

When I'm faced with a bunker shot that I must hit high and stop quickly, I revert to a method advocated by Claude Harmon, the former Winged Foot teacher. It can work for you, too.

At address, set the blade of your sand wedge open and place your hands on the club in a weak position, turned counterclockwise or to the left. Play the ball forward, which puts your hands behind the clubhead.

On the backswing, cock the club up quickly and fan it open by cupping your left wrist. From there, swing down into the sand behind the ball as hard as you want, releasing your hands fully. You want to feel that the clubhead is passing your hands through impact. You must do this, in fact, or risk shanking the shot.

Because you started from such an open clubface position at the top, the club won't dig into the sand. Instead, it will pass nicely under the ball and you'll get a high shot that always lands dead.

Strange set a new PGA Tour record for earnings in a single season with $542,321 in 1985. He won the Honda Classic, Panasonic-Las Vegas Invitational and Canadian Open in the process. Has won a total of eight tournaments and $1,951,848 in his nine-year career on the tour, following a sparkling amateur career at Wake Forest, where he won the individual 1974 NCAA title and was named college player of the year.

Practice without a ball to improve sand savvy

A good way to think about bunker shots is that wherever the sand goes, so goes the ball. If you make the sand go high, the ball will go high; if you make the sand go low, the ball will go low, too.

To make the ball go high, you can use "the trick," which is what Strange's shot is called on tour. Cocking the club open creates more loft, which will make the sand bounce higher off the club. Therefore the ball will go higher. The clubhead passing the hands quickly will also lift the sand higher. It's unbelievable how high you can shoot the ball up in the air with this method.

A fun way to practice your sand shots is with sand only—no ball. Take some swings and just splash the sand up in the air toward the flagstick. After a while, put a rock or walnut on top of the sand and repeat the procedure. Finally, put a ball on the sand and see if you can duplicate the ease and effectiveness of the no-ball and small-ball shots. Soon your bunker fears will be eliminated.

Jim McQueen

Restrict lower body for fairway bunker success

By LARRY MIZE

The common fault in fairway bunkers, even for good players, is swinging too hard. Result: your feet slip in the sand, your body moves and you mis-hit the shot.

To guard against this, I plant my feet in the sand, then make a deliberate attempt to restrict my lower-body movement. This shortens my swing and makes it nice and compact. I stay steady over the ball, make a smooth swing and contact the ball first, nipping it nicely off the sand.

To counteract the shorter, more compact swing, I take a half-club to a club more than the distance normally would call for. But if there is a big lip on the bunker, make sure you take a club with enough loft to get over that lip. You're better off playing short of the green and trying to get it up and down from there than going for it with a club that's too straight-faced.

Born in Augusta, Ga., Mize won $231,041 in 1985, his best season to date on the money list. Widely praised as possessor of one of the smoothest swings in the game, Mize won the 1983 Danny Thomas-Memphis Classic with a 25-foot birdie putt on the 72nd hole. He finished second in the 1986 Tournament Players Championship.

Your "measurement" at address should be same at impact

I believe Larry's advice is exceptional for all players. The most important thing in a fairway bunker is to establish your measurements to the ball at address—such as your height, amount of knee flex and your arms and club extension—and then reestablish those measurements at impact. In planting your feet, dig them in where they won't slip. This will lower your swing arc, so you need to raise it back up by choking down on the club. When you restrict your lower-body action, you will reduce your ability to shift to the left side, so play the ball farther back in your stance than you would with a fairway iron—even with the center of your body would be good. This will allow you to catch the ball while slightly descending with the club, thereby reducing the probability of a fat shot which is the most penal mistake you can make in a fairway bunker. You're trying to get out of the trap with distance, so you'd much rather catch the shot "thin" than fat.

It's important to spend some time practicing this "trouble shot," as well as others. It will make it less troublesome when you have to play the shot in competition.

SHORT GAME/SAND

Jim McQueen

From greenside rough, pitch a "knuckleball"

By WAYNE LEVI

Coming into the final hole at the Buick Open in '83, I was in a tough spot. I had a very shaky lead over Calvin Peete and Isao Aoki, and I was in the rough 30 feet from the green and 90 feet from the pin. For this shot I use a sand wedge.

Open the clubface and take the club back outside, on a steep arc, with a one-piece motion. It's basically an arm swing. There's very little wrist break and you want to keep your body as still as possible.

On the downswing, slide the club under the ball along the same out-to-in path. The ball will come out like a knuckleball—floating high, landing softly and stopping fairly quickly.

It worked for me on this occasion. I got up and down in two to win the tournament. So can you if you'll practice.

A consistent but underrated player, Levi has won more than $220,000 on the PGA Tour in three of the last four years. He has amassed $1,292,888 and eight wins in a nine-year career, including the 1983 Buick Open and the 1985 Georgia Pacific-Atlanta Classic.

Keep the "knuckles under" to hit the "knuckleball"

There are two key words in Wayne's tip—"under" and "knuckle." To execute this shot, your attention must be concentrated on getting the club *under* the ball. If you try to hit down on the ball, it will come out too low and too fast. If you try to "scoop" the ball, the odds of a mis-hit are greatly increased. The answer, then, is to think of swinging *under*.

A foolproof way of keeping the loft on the club necessary to hit a high, soft pitch from high grass is to keep the *knuckles* of the right hand under throughout the shot. This will allow the bounce of the club to get under the ball and keep the club from digging into the grass.

So remember, "knuckles under" to hit the "knuckleball."

PUTTING

PUTTING

Pop your putts

By BRUCE LIETZKE

Many of us on tour consider acceleration perhaps the most important factor in putting, especially for the short putts. Tom Watson and Jack Nicklaus are a couple of players besides myself who come quickly to mind. We use almost a "pop" stroke to get the ball to the hole.

I've devised a practice drill that develops muscle memory to encourage acceleration on the short putts. I first mark where I want to place the ball by sticking a tee in the green just outside my putting path. Then I put another tee in the green directly behind the ball on my backswing path—five or six inches back for a five-foot putt, another inch or so back for a 10-footer. For a 15-footer I'll put the tee about eight inches back, but never any farther. Any putt longer than that requires more feel instead of a "pop" stroke.

When I take the putter back, I try not to touch the tee. This forces me to pause and then to exaggerate the acceleration of my forward stroke to get the ball to the hole. I go from the shorter to the longer putts, then do away with the tee and continue practicing my accelerating stroke for a few minutes to ingrain the feel without artificial help.

Since joining the PGA Tour in 1975 Lietzke has won 10 tournaments and $1,986,368 in prize money, ranking him 11th on the all-time list. He is one of the foremost proponents of the cross-handed putting stroke.

PUTTING

Take this "pop test" to see if you're under-or-overaccelerating

Most good putters "swing" the putter. That is, they don't push or overaccelerate it, nor do they decelerate. I would say that a putter that is "swung" would have equal amounts of backswing and follow-through, just like a pendulum. If you decelerate the putter, your backswing would be longer than your follow-through. If you overaccelerate it, your follow-through would be longer than your backswing. You can be a reasonably good long putter with a somewhat decelerating stroke, but you probably wouldn't be a very good short putter. If you overaccelerate, chances are you would be better with short putts than with long ones. The best *all-round* putters have a balanced stroke.

To develop a balanced stroke, set up to a level 12-foot putt and place tees adjacent and parallel to your target line 12 inches behind the ball and 12 inches in front of it. Then hit some putts and notice how far back and through your putter goes. If you tend to decelerate (your follow-through is shorter than your backswing), it's appropriate to practice "popping" your putts as Lietzke suggests. However, if you overaccelerate and are already "popping" your putts, you should be more concerned with "smoothing out" your stroke.

PUTTING

Keep putter soled flat for smoother rolls

By PATTY SHEEHAN

When my putter goes awry, it's often because I've allowed my hands to get in too close to my body at address. When that happens, I get the toe of the putter off the ground and start to push and pull putts off line. I have to remember to keep my hands away from my body a little bit so that the putter sits flat.

When the putter is properly soled, I have a much better chance of rolling the ball into the cup. Once I'm certain that the putter's in place, getting the ball to roll consistently and smoothly is what I work on.

Sheehan has won 14 events in her first five years on the LPGA Tour and, at press time had added the '86 Sarasota and Kyocera Inamori Classics to that record. In 1985, she finished in the top 10 nine consecutive times. The 1981 Rookie of the Year won the LPGA Championship in both 1983 and '84 and has been in the top five on the money list each of the past four years.

PUTTING

Adjust your putter to your body, not vice versa

Patty's tip is absolutely correct. However, I'd like to add one comment. Just as many golfers handicap their putting with improper technique, others do themselves a disservice by not using a putter that complements their body and setup. It's important to have the putter soled correctly, as Patty says, but it's even more important to have a properly fitted putter properly soled.

Too often, people accommodate their setup or swings to clubs not designed for them, rather than buying equipment that would enhance their game. To find out if your putter fits you, take your stance with the putter soled. If when you do this, your eyes are over the line and your hands are under your shoulders, you have a good fit. If not, adjust that $50 putter to your million-dollar body—not vice versa.

PUTTING

Jim McQueen

Purposely "toe" putts in practice to smooth stroke

By D.A. WEIBRING

Ideally, you want to hit the ball on the sweet spot of your putter every time, but that doesn't always happen. Even the better players get into bad habits like watching the putter blade going back or playing the ball too far forward in the stance.

To guard against these tendencies, a few guys on tour like to practice hitting putts with the toe of the putter. It's something you can do very quickly before you go out to play, just by turning the putter 90 degrees counterclockwise and making a good, slow stroke. Of course, it will only work with a blade putter.

Because the margin for error is so much smaller, it helps you to slow down your stroke so you can contact the ball solidly. If you are misaligned or are watching the blade instead of the ball, your mistakes will be magnified and you'll be forced to make the necessary adjustments. Using the toe can really help your rhythm and concentration before a round and pay substantial dividends when you get out on the course.

Winner of the 1979 Quad Cities Open Weibring has earned $728,029 in his nine years on the PGA Tour, $153,079 of that total in 1985. He finished second to Calvin Peete in the 1985 Tournament Players Championship and tied for eighth in his first trip to the British Open.

PLAYING

PRACTICE

Know the difference between practice and warm-up

There are tremendous training aids to help you practice putting the ball precisely. There are putters on the market that have prongs protruding on either side of the sweet spot that squirt the ball way off line in the event of a mis-hit, and there's a putter with a head shaped like a large metal Ping-Pong ball that will only produce straight shots when the equator of the putter hits the equator of the ball. Hitting the ball with the toe of the putter like D.A. does requires the same type of precision. As I said, these are great training devices—but I would not recommend using them immediately prior to teeing off.

There is a vital difference between practicing and warming up for a round. Practice is used to learn or relearn a certain skill and any aids that help are encouraged. However, a warm-up is designed to get you ready to *play* golf and you should be trying to get into a playing "mode" and feel good about your game. That is, warm up with clubs that are easy to hit, use familiar swings (don't give yourself a lesson) and get thinking about the conditions you are about to meet—are the greens especially fast today? Using aids at the inappropriate time will produce doubts and frustration; for instance, if you keep mis-hitting the ball with the toe of the putter. So train during practice time and think about playing during warm-up time.

PUTTING

Exaggerate follow-through on practice putts

By HOLLIS STACY

To win majors like the U.S. Open, you've got to make short putts. They save pars and get you birdies.

Because they are so important, however, I sometimes find myself concentrating solely on the backstroke of these putts—and forgetting all about the follow-through, which is a mistake. My sister, a good amateur player, tells me it begins on my practice stroke. I take a long backstroke and then stop the blade at the ball. You've probably done the same thing. After a practice stroke like that, is it any wonder we decelerate on the putt itself?

To avoid decelerating on short putts, try making your practice stroke the way you want your real stroke to be—with a shorter backstroke and a fuller follow-through. It doesn't hurt to make an exaggerated follow-through on the practice stroke—two or three times the length of the backstroke—just to remind yourself to stroke the ball through to the hole.

So if you're taking the putter back three inches, follow through six inches on the practice stroke. On the putt itself, just remember that feeling and stroke the ball right into the hole.

Stacy's 17 tournament wins in 12 years on the LPGA Tour include the 1977, 1978 and 1984 U.S. Women's Open. Her tour earnings through 1985 total $1,047,480. A record-setting junior golfer, Stacy captured the USGA Junior Girls' Championship three years in a row (1969-1971), giving her a career total of six USGA national championships.

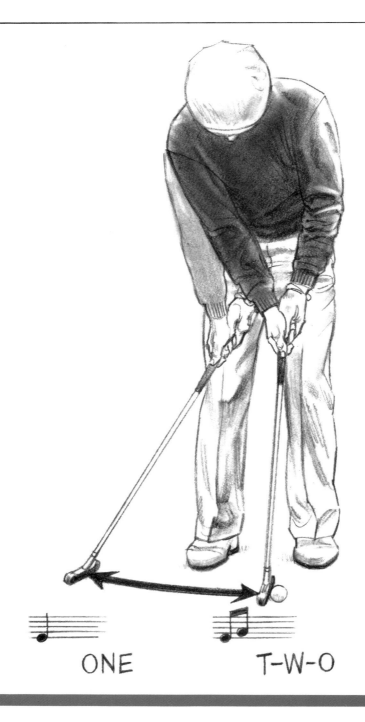

ONE   T-W-O

Develop a balanced stroke by working on its "beat"

One big precaution about Hollis' tip: note that she says *practice*. It's especially good for people who decelerate during the stroke. In practice it will help you develop a stroke that is balanced in length which is best for all putts—because the putter is neither "pushed" nor stopped but "swung." Any change in pressure required to push or stop the putter will often change the clubface or path, causing mis-hit putts.

However, thinking about the length of the stroke is not a good way to putt. Thinking about the "beat" of the stroke is. Try counting 1–2 as you putt. The beat of the backswing and downswing

should be the same. I've had success telling my students to think in musical terms—if you've got a high pitch (alto) then you should have an alto backswing and an alto downswing. If you decelerate, you might be alto on the backswing and a baritone on the downswing, or if you overaccelerate you might be just the opposite—an alto back and soprano down.

To correct these problems, you should think of reversing roles—being a baritone on the backswing and an alto to speed up the downswing and avoid decelerating. Get your beat down and you'll get your putts down, too.

IV
STRATEGY/
MENTAL

Jim McQueen

A hurricane plan for wind: Don't panic; swing easy

By LANNY WADKINS

It was very windy all week during the 1982 Buick Open, and my ability to handle it was a key factor in my winning the tournament. The wind blew in four different directions the first three rounds. The last day, it turned around and blew the same way it had the first round, when I shot 66.

Many people panic and try to fight the wind. I was like that for a long time, but I finally realized that if you play the game 30 weeks a year, the wind is going to blow 20 of them. So you might as well get used to it and be patient.

The key to playing in the wind is that you can't let it control you.

Play within yourself, and don't force your shots. Play the ball back a little in your stance with the irons and tee it lower with the driver. Then just stay in balance—swing easier and hit it solidly. I never try to swing hard when the wind is blowing. By hitting the ball easier, you can keep it under control and down, where the wind can't catch it as easily. I also take more club than normal, even in crosswinds.

So the next time you're playing in the wind, swing easy and just concentrate on hitting the ball solidly. You'll be pleasantly surprised how little the wind will affect your shots—and your score.

Wadkins was named PGA Player of the Year in 1985 after winning three tournaments and finishing second in earnings ($446,893) and scoring average (70.44). The former Wake Forest standout won the U.S. Amateur title in 1970 and counts the 1977 PGA Championship at Pebble Beach among his 15 professional victories.

Reduce the amount of spin in wind to keep the ball under control

Lanny's got a good plan for the wind, and it has served him well over the years. It sounds to me like he got a lot of his information from Byron Nelson, one of the great wind players of all time. Keep in mind that when the ball is hit, spin is produced. There are two types of spin: underspin and sidespin. Your goal in controlling the ball in the wind is to reduce the spin. This will keep the ball from upshooting into the wind and avoid sidespin, which is accentuated in windy conditions.

There are three things that can help you reduce spin:

1) Use more club. This will necessitate less speed, and less spin will result.

2) Choke down. This will in effect "stiffen" the shaft, creating a lower ball flight.

3) Swing easy. This will increase your chances of achieving solid contact, thereby reducing the possibility of sidespin.

Keep these three keys in mind and you, too, can become a "wind-cheater."

Play to a partner's strengths and "no apologies"

By JOHN MAHAFFEY and JoANNE CARNER

The philosophy that we used to win the mixed-team championship—and that you should use to succeed in golf's game of doubles—is to play to each other's strengths. For us, strategy comes into play mostly on the par 5s. The Penney format uses the Chapman system—we both drive, then hit each other's second shot. After that, we pick the best ball to play and alternate from there on into the cup.

JoAnne's short game is very good, and one of her best shots is the 50-or 60-yard wedge. So on holes like No. 16 (see illustration), a medium-length par 5, if JoAnne hits a good drive, John can go for the green in two and get her up there as close as possible. On the other hand, if JoAnne is hitting the second shot, she can lay farther back so John could have the full shot he prefers into the green. That's the key—putting your partner in the position from which he or she is most comfortable. On a short par 4, JoAnne might tee off with a 3-wood instead of a driver to leave John far enough back.

A lot of couples play mixed events at the club level and end up in arguments. On tour, we invoke the "no apologies" rule, which is our answer to the "I'm sorry, dear" syndrome you find so many couples falling into. If one of us flubs a shot, we simply forget about it and go onto the next shot. Like love, mixed-team play means never having to say you're sorry.

Mahaffey has won over $2,000,000 in 15 years on the PGA Tour, including the 1986 TPC. In the 1978 PGA Championship at Oakmont he beat Tom Watson and Jerry Pate in a playoff and was named Golf Digest's Comeback Player of the Year. JoAnne Carner is a member of the LPGA Hall of Fame with $1,931,189 in earnings and 42 career victories through 1985. She was one of the finest women amateurs in golf history, capturing five U.S. Amateur titles. The two teamed together to win the 1982 JC Penney Classic.

Treat yourself the same way you would a friend or playing partner

The hidden message in this "team tip" is that it applies to singles play as well. Putting yourself in position to use your preferred shot and standard swing as often as possible is the key to consistency. If you are constantly having to change speeds, tempos, shapes, trajectories, etc., you will find yourself using your weaknesses instead of your strengths. As the venerable teacher Harvey Penick puts it: "Pralines and cream are nice every now and then, but plain vanilla is best for a steady diet."

As for the "no apologies" rule, that too should apply to individual stroke play. How often do you hear yourself saying, "You dumb $-*\&\frac{1}{4}\,{}^{s}!$, how could you hit that shot!"? You certainly wouldn't say that to a friend or partner. As sports psychologists advise: "Be your own best friend," giving yourself encouragement and support during a round. If you treat yourself with the same kindness you give others, you'll enjoy yourself—and the game—a lot more.

Think with head, not heart, down the stretch

By COREY PAVIN

When I won my first tournament, in South Africa in 1983, I got so psyched up that I became very tired during the round. Going into the last round at Houston in 1984, I was tied for second and didn't want to get too pumped up again, so my thoughts were to keep everything slow and smooth.

I consciously walked a little slower and took a little more time than I usually do. By thinking "slow and smooth," I was able to maintain control, to make decisions rationally instead of emotionally.

This really paid off for me at Houston on the 17th hole on Sun-day. I had taken a two-shot lead coming into this tough par 4 when I drove into the left rough. That didn't leave me much of a shot to the green, unless I wanted to try for the very right corner. I decided to play the percentages, so that the *worst* I could do would be to make a bogey. I played my second shot so the worst place it could end up would be in the front bunker, which it did. I got it out to within eight feet and missed the par putt, but that was OK.

I had avoided the trap of getting carried away by emotions and trying something I couldn't do. I parred 18 to win by one and had enough energy left to celebrate.

Named Golf Digest's Rookie of the Year in 1984 when he won $260,536 on the PGA Tour, Pavin's year was highlighted by a victory in the Houston Coca-Cola Open. In 1985 he won $367,506 and the Colonial National Invitation, and got off to a quick start in 1986 with his third tour win at the Hawaiian Open.

Develop a repeating routine to relieve the pressure

Imagine driving a dark, winding road late at night. If you've never driven it before, you'll have to make some maneuvers of which you're unsure, and you'll probably be uptight and nervous doing so. If you don't play a lot of competitive golf, being in contention for any sort of prize will produce the same feelings.

But if you have driven that dark, winding road to and from work every day for the past 10 years, it becomes routine because you're familiar with its idiosyncracies.

Good players feel fear, too, but when the nerves threaten to freeze the brain, they swing using the same routine so they go on "automatic pilot." They have the same basic physical and mental approach to every shot—they plan it the same way, they step up to the ball the same way, they waggle the same way and consequently, their shots are not affected as much by pressure. And they have the ability to make pre- and in-round adjustments like the "slowing down" Corey keyed on to win the 1984 Houston tournament.

Develop your own routine and practice it under calm conditions so you can negotiate that dark, winding road called "pressure."

Sometimes you should forget the wedge

By BRAD FAXON

Too often, golfers choose a wedge for an approach shot without considering the conditions.

When you have a tight lie, a lot of wind, or a very firm green, it's safer to "knock down" a 6-iron rather than try to hit a wedge.

The key is keeping your hands ahead of the clubhead through the impact area.

Address the ball with your knees flexed and *keep* them flexed. Set your hands ahead of the ball, and play the ball back in your stance. Your hands should be on a vertical line with your left knee.

Let your right shoulder control the tempo of the swing. A key to keep in mind: Try to return to your address position at impact. A way to insure this is by maintaining the angle between your right arm and the shaft. That keeps your hands ahead of the ball—and keeps the ball on a low trajectory.

An outstanding amateur at Furman University, Faxon won 11 collegiate tournaments and was named to the All-American team in both 1982 and 1983. He turned professional in 1983 and has won $118,500 in his first two years on the PGA Tour.

Use the "strike and hold" drill to keep the club low to the ground

An effective way to think of controlling the trajectory of your shots is to remember that the height of the ball is influenced by the arc of your swing. If the head of the club comes up very quickly after impact, then the ball will go high. If the head of the club stays low to the ground after impact, the ball will stay low. Therefore, in playing the "knockdown," your goal is to keep the clubhead low after impact.

A drill I learned to accomplish this came from Bob Toski, dean of the Golf Digest Schools. It is called the "strike and hold" drill. That is, strike the ball and try to hold the club low after impact—don't finish the swing by coming up and around on your usual follow-through. This will keep the knees flexed and create the low, "knockdown" shot you're looking for.

Don't play Superman in the tall grass

By ROGER MALTBIE

Some players panic when they get into super-high rough. Others don't take it seriously enough. The main thing is, don't be too much of a hero. If the lie is bad, take your medicine, get the ball to the fairway and try to make par from there.

On the shot itself, open your stance and open the clubface. Pick the club up more abruptly on your backswing so that the angle you come into the ball will be steeper. Take it back slightly more outside the target line than usual to encourage a fade. Remember, you want to get as little grass as possible between the clubface and the ball because that grass will slow the club down and close the face, causing a low, uncontrolled hook.

Use common sense. You can't play normal shots from deep rough. That's why they call it "rough."

Won two tournaments in his 1976 rookie year but only one between then and 1985, when he had his best year ever with victories in the Manufacturers Hanover Westchester Classic and NEC World Series of Golf for $360,554 in earnings. Those efforts earned Maltbie Golf Digest's Male Comeback Player of the Year award.

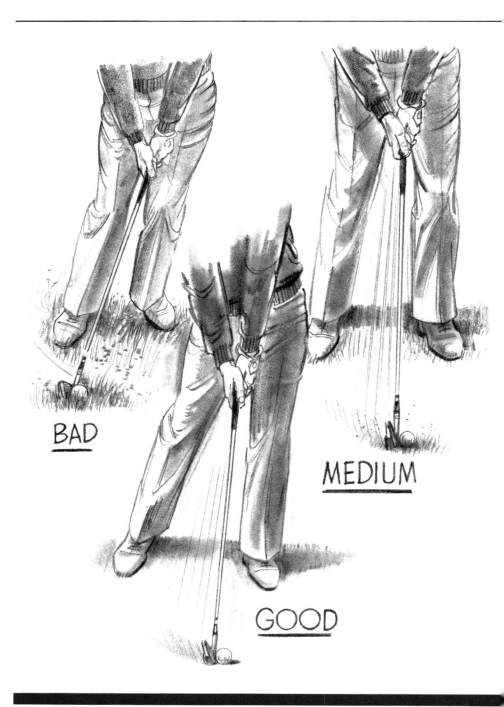

BAD

MEDIUM

GOOD

Grade your lie in the rough before plotting escape route

I try to get my students, especially tour players, to learn to "grade" their lie in the rough. A lie where the ball is sitting on top of the rough is called a good lie. A ball sitting down in the grass, but not on the ground, is a medium lie. And a ball sitting down on the ground deep in the rough is called—you guessed it—a bad lie.

You use different strategies depending on the lie; in other words, the lie dictates the shot. The good lie can be positioned like a driver, as the ball is sitting on a "tee" of grass. Move it forward in your stance and "sweep" the ball cleanly toward your target.

A medium lie will get some grass between the club and ball, creating a "flyer" when contact is made. Play it like you would a shot from a good lie but allow for more roll and distance.

A bad lie will react like a ball hit by a club with three headcovers on it. The only sensible solution is to plan on taking two shots to reach your target, and cut your losses by making your next shot as easy as possible.

Know your partner—and don't overcoach

By FRED COUPLES with JAN STEPHENSON

The key to success in team play is finding a partner you are comfortable with. Golf is hard enough without trying to team with someone who gets on your nerves.

Fortunately for me, Jan is very easy to team with. We paired well because I drive the ball pretty far and she's a great iron player. You want a partner who complements your game that way.

One mistake I think club players make is automatically assuming they need to coach their partners at every turn. They think they have to give pep talks, read putts and help with club selection. That puts too much pressure on most people.

My advice is to talk these things over before you tee it up. It will pay off in the end.

A blossoming star on the PGA Tour, Couples has won $872,124 in his first five seasons, capped by the 1984 Tournament Players Championship. Known as "Boom Boom" for his prodigious tee shots, Couples ranked No. 1 in driving distance in cumulative rankings from 1980-1985 with a 273.9 yard-per-drive average. He teamed with LPGA star Jan Stephenson to win the 1983 JC Penney Mixed Team Classic.

Remember, not everyone wants—or needs—advice

In general, this is great advice. The key to remember is that everyone is different, plays differently and reacts to different stimuli. In club play, there is sometimes a big differential in handicaps among players on the same team or in the same group. In such cases, the high handicapper often wants to be led or "coached" by the more experienced player in things like green reading, strategy and club selection. I know when I play with people, they like me to say, for example, "Why don't you play this tee shot down the left side and let the slope roll it back into the fairway?"

On the other hand, if you are playing with a person of compar-able skill, you may want to plan your round beforehand and give advice only when asked. Look at Jack Nicklaus and Tom Watson. They are different types of putters (Watson's a charger, Nicklaus more of a lag putter), and because of this they read greens differently. Say you asked your partner—a Nicklaus-type putter—to read a putt. He might say: "It will break three inches to the left." But when you —a Watson-type putter—put your aggressive stroke on it, the putt probably won't break that much.

That's why, as Fred and Jan say, you've got to know your partner and know when not to overcoach.

Visualize to improve long-iron shots

By DAVID EDWARDS

Even accomplished players sometimes cringe when they have to hit a long-iron shot, especially under pressure. Yet many of the finishing holes on the tour's Western swing, including the 18th at Riviera (where I won in 1984) and the 17th at Pebble Beach, require accurate long-iron shots.

When the heat is on and I'm looking at a 3- or 4-iron shot, I picture my brother Danny's swing before I hit the shot. I've always admired the effortlessness of his swing, and visualizing it reminds me that the club will hit the ball a long way—*I* don't have to. This helps me maintain my normal tempo and balance.

You might use the same technique. Find a player (a friend or a pro) whose swing you find especially fluid. Think of him or her the next time you're faced with one of those difficult long-iron shots.

Edwards was the 1978 NCAA individual winner and has won $596,978 in seven years on the PGA Tour. He won the 1980 Walt Disney World National Team Championship (with older brother Danny) and the 1984 Los Angeles Open with a final-round 64 (seven under par) at Riviera Country Club.

Fairway woods a good alternative to those tough-to-hit long irons

Hitting long irons consistently well is a skill possessed by very few. The clubhead on a long iron is much lighter than those on the shorter irons. If you are familiar with Einstein's theorem of energy equals mass times velocity squared $(E = MV^2)$, then you should realize there must be an incremental increase in speed to make the ball go correspondingly longer. That's why a lot of golfers, especially ladies, can't hit their long irons any longer than their middle irons. A good substitute is the lofted fairway wood, which is usually easier for the average golfer to hit.

However, if you have the capability to use long irons, visualization is certainly the key. Some images I've found helpful in coaching long-iron swings are as follows:

"Clip the grass out from under the ball."

"Swing the club like a bucket of water."

"Be the first player in history who isn't in a hurry to finish his swing."

V
SPECIALTY

SPECIALTY

Relax and release to hit a soft draw

By KEITH FERGUS

The critical play in my win at Atlanta in 1982 was *not* my birdie to beat Ray Floyd on the first playoff hole. Instead it came much earlier in the final round, on the 431-yard fourth hole.

I had just three-putted the third hole, was four shots back of leader Larry Nelson and needed a boost. I had driven the ball within 145 yards of the flag, which was tucked into the left corner of a green bordered by water in front and on the left. The putting surface was only 20 feet deep in that area.

To get the ball close I felt I had to draw the ball in softly from right to left with an 8-iron. For a shot like this, I position the ball just back of center in my stance, close the clubface a little, try to stay behind the ball and release my hands through impact, letting the clubface do most of the work. I find that relaxing my shoulders and grip helps me do this—it reduces the tension in my hands, arms and upper body and promotes a better turn.

This time it all worked. I hit the shot about eight feet from the hole and made the putt for a birdie. I finished with a 69 for 273 to get in the playoff with Floyd.

A three-time All-American at the University of Houston, Fergus has won three times on the PGA Tour—the 1981 Memorial, 1982 Georgia-Pacific Atlanta Classic and 1983 Bob Hope Classic. Two of those wins came in playoffs—over Ray Floyd in Atlanta and Rex Caldwell in the Hope.

Swinging a bucket of water can help you control fade or draw

Hitting the shot Keith did in winning at Atlanta is probably the dream of many high handicappers who have a tendency to slice the ball. An image I use to help these people learn to control their ball's curvature and eventually draw it might help you, too.

Pretend you are holding a bucket of water. To hit the straight shot, you would never spill the water— the bucket would stay upright on the backswing and on the follow-through.

To draw the ball, feel like you would spill the water to the left on your follow-through. And to fade the ball, feel like you would spill the water to the right on your follow-through. You can even practice this motion by swinging a bucket that's partially filled with some water or sand.

In other words, spill the water in the direction you want the ball to go but be sure to aim for it!

Jim McQueen

Try my favorite fringe benefit: the "bellied wedge"

By GARY KOCH

One of my favorite short-game tricks is what I call the "bellied wedge." It's useful from higher grass just beyond the fringe or when the ball is on the fringe resting against the higher grass.

I use a sand wedge and hit it with my regular putting stroke. I use my basic putting setup and reverse overlap grip and make sure that the ball is at least in the middle of my stance, maybe even slightly back of middle. I address the ball with the leading edge square, aimed at the ball's equator. Then I strike it as close as possible to that equator—smack in the belly—with my putting motion, using a wrist-free stroke with the arms swinging from the shoulders.

With this shot, you don't ever feel like you'll stick the club in the ground behind the ball and barely move it. By making sure I hit the middle of the ball, I know it's going to come out and I know it's going to run. The other advantage is accuracy; it's easy to get the ball started on the line you want it on. The shorter the distance, the easier it is to use. I generally hit it anywhere up to 30 feet from the flag; beyond that, it's tough to judge how hard to hit it.

One warning: perfecting this shot requires a lot of practice to determine how hard you need to hit it to make the ball go the distance you want. But once you get it right, I'm sure you'll want to "belly" up for more.

Koch won the Florida state junior championship in three consecutive years (1968–1970) and was on the 1973 NCAA title-winning team at University of Florida. After a lean stretch on the PGA Tour, the Florida native found his stride in 1984, winning two tournaments in five weeks—at San Diego and Bay Hill—coming from six shots behind in both before prevailing in playoffs.

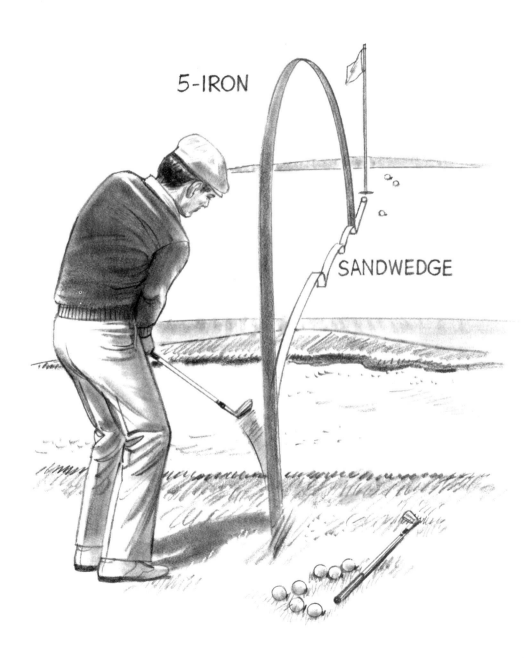

5-IRON

SANDWEDGE

Expand your imagination through practice improvisation

Gary's technique is fine and I have nothing to add to the playing of this shot. But I feel there's an even more important lesson to be learned from this tip.

One thing I've noticed about all the tour-caliber players with whom I've worked is that they have great imagination for creating and executing different kinds of shots.

Learning this "bellied wedge" shot took a lot of imagination. It also required plenty of practice. One rule we should all live by is to never try something on a golf course you haven't practiced successfully first.

A fun and effective way to expand your imagination and understanding of the fundamentals of shotmaking is to practice hitting high, soft pitches over a bunker with a 5-iron (some may recall the "One Club Challenge" matches a few years ago, where great improvisers like Seve Ballesteros and Lee Trevino actually had to do this in competition). Then try hitting some low shots with a sand wedge.

You'll soon be able to picture the kinds of shots you are trying to hit.

Jim McQueen

Choke down, swing easier to hit the fairway driver

By GIL MORGAN

Hitting your driver off the fairway can be advantageous in certain situations—when you can't fly the ball all the way to the green, when you need to keep a shot low into the wind and occasionally even out of the short rough when the ball is sitting up and you have a "flyer" situation. It works well on hard, fast fairways like the ones you find out West, in Texas and in Florida.

You can't carry the ball as far with your driver as you can with your 3-wood—at least I can't—but the ball will hit the ground hot and travel farther over all, so you should only play the shot on a hole when there is no trouble in front of the green. And, of course, you must have a good lie or an uphill lie so you can get the clubface on the ball. The opportunity is most likely to occur on a par 5 and sometimes on a long par 4.

To play the shot, I choke down on the club about an inch and a half and move the ball back in my stance, positioning it where I would for a fairway wood. Your angle of approach must not be as steep as it is with a fairway wood or iron, so be sure you don't get the ball too far back. I then swing a little shorter and a little easier to make sure I make good contact. If I miss, I want to miss the shot thin instead of fat, because I'll get a lot more out of it.

Morgan has been a solid, consistent performer and has won $1,786,219 and six events in 12 years on the PGA Tour. He was named Golf Digest's Most Improved Male Professional in 1978 after he won the Glen Campbell-Los Angeles Open and the World Series of Golf, and finished second on the money list. He won the first two tournaments of 1983 and passed $300,000 in earnings that year, a career first.

SPECIALTY

YOU NEED A SHALLOW-
FACED DRIVER . . . . . .   A GOOD
FAIRWAY LIE...

...TO HIT DRIVER OFF THE FAIRWAY

Use driver with caution— fairway wood a safer bet

This is a shot that has several applications but more importantly, it has several limitations. You've got to have the right club, the right lie and the right skill level to be able to pull it off. For most people to get the ball airborne, the center of gravity of the club must get below the equator of the ball. Therefore, there are some types of driver clubs that are not feasible to hit from the fairway. Deep-faced drivers or drivers with limited loft should not be used. The best kind are shallow-faced drivers, high-lofted drivers or drivers that are backweighted.

Hitting a driver from the fairway also requires a good lie. There must be some air under the ball. Hitting the ball off a tight lie is too risky— it leaves no margin for error.

Finally, hitting the driver from the fairway requires a high degree of skill. You must be able to create a reasonable amount of clubhead speed to get enough "lift spin" to get the ball airborne. Because of these limitations, I recommend that most of you opt for a fairway wood and rely on your short game to save your score. There is nothing wrong with giving up a little distance and making up for it with a strong short game.

Jim McQueen

Hood the clubface for a sharp hook

By CHIP BECK

Most of the time when you've hit the ball off line you have to be smart about it and just get the ball back safely in play. There are times, though, when being able to hit a very sharp hook can get you out of a tight spot and onto the green.

The key to this shot is to align your body along the line that you want to start the ball, but to hood the clubface so that it is aiming where you want the ball to end up. I play the ball back slightly in my stance, but that is really the only change I make. I let the hooded clubface take care of the rest.

Keep in mind that this shot will carry and roll farther than a normal shot. For example, my normal 5-iron travels about 180 yards. With this shot it goes 200 yards and will roll slightly when it hits the green. The more hook you play, the more roll you will get. In the 1982 Buick Open I had a 180-yard shot to the pin but had to hook it almost 80 yards around the trees. Believe me, when I saw that ball end up near the flag, I became the world's leading disciple of this shot.

A three-time All-American at the University of Georgia, Beck was named the school's senior athlete of the year in 1978—the first time a golfer had ever been so honored. He joined the PGA Tour in 1979 and has since won more than $500,000.

Know your normal tendencies to avoid creating more trouble

Chip's tip is simple to understand and quite correct technically. However, there are a couple of cautions I'd like to add.

First of all, keep in mind that Chip's basic shot is reasonably straight. Therefore, the alignment adjustments he makes will produce the "quick hook." But, if your basic shot tendency is not straight, you'll need to be careful. For example, if you normally come over the ball, you would pull it into the tree with that closed clubface. To avoid that, you would need to aim farther right.

If you normally slice your ball, the closed clubface will merely straighten the shot rather than produce the tree-escaping hook, so you need to accentuate the closed clubface even more at address. And if you already hook the ball, you might hook it too quickly, right into the tree and more trouble.

The best way to learn what's available to you is to go practice this shot—hit balls around, over and under trees—and find out first-hand what *you* have to do.

Play ball back, delay release for low, long shot

By JAY HAAS

I was tied for the lead during the third round of the 1982 Texas Open when I hit my tee shot left on the 460-yard 15th hole. I wound up under a tree, facing a 200-yard shot that I had to keep low under the tree and still carry at least 170 yards to reach the green. I also had to draw the ball a little. Fortunately I could take a full swing.

For this shot you want to play the ball back in your stance, at least to the middle and maybe farther back, depending on how low you must keep it. This puts your hands ahead of the ball and promotes the descending blow you need.

You must delay the release of your hands as you come into impact, finishing low with your arms extended. You should practice to acquire a feel for just how much you delay or release them depending on whether you need a fade, a straight shot or a draw. But remember, your main concern is keeping the ball low.

I chose a 4-iron and played the shot perfectly, ending up with a 30-foot putt that I almost made. But my par in such a pressure situation pumped me up. I went on to shoot 67 to tie Curtis Strange for the lead, then shot 65 the next day to win by three.

A five-time winner in nine years on the PGA Tour, Haas has earned over $100,000 in each of the last seven seasons. An All-American at Wake Forest in 1975 and '76, Haas is the nephew of former Masters champion Bob Goalby.

SPECIALTY

UNDER TREE SHOT OVER BROOK TO GREEN 200 YDS. AWAY, 4-IRON CARRIES 170 YDS. AND RUNS 30.

NO BROOK, 2-IRON CARRIES 140 YDS. AND RUNS 60.

Another way to hit it low: Choose a less-lofted club

The physics of hitting the ball low are simple enough. The less effective loft on the club, the lower the ball will go. There are two ways to reduce effective loft. The easiest is to *choose* less loft in your club selection. For example, Jay could've chosen a 2-iron for his shot and hit the ball low enough to stay under the trees. If he had plenty of room to run the ball onto the green, this would've been the easiest option.

However, he says he had to keep the ball low, carry it 170 yards but stop it within 30 yards after it landed. This required a different way of reducing loft. He took a more-lofted club (4-iron) and effectively turned it into a 2-iron by playing the ball back in his stance. This produced a sharper angle into the ball, creating more backspin which made the ball carry farther and stop quicker.

Hit it low either way. Just remember your physics.

SPECIALTY

Eliminate danger off the tee with a 1-iron

By JOHN FOUGHT

Because so many holes require pinpoint shot placement off the tee, the 1-iron is a valuable club for a player who can handle it. Too often a player will automatically reach for the driver on every par-4 and par-5 hole when that might not be the correct choice at all. The 1-iron might be a more effective option.

Golf course architects often try to tempt you into playing to the tightest, most dangerous areas to get what you think will be the best shot into the green. They plant fairway bunkers 240 to 280 yards out, or they put water there or squeeze the fairway in until it's barely wide enough to walk through. Hitting a driver into areas like that is just asking for trouble.

I eliminate the risk simply by taking a 1-iron—it might even be a 2-or 3-iron if the hole is short enough—and laying up short of the danger. I look for the widest area to play into, not the tightest, and often that wide area is one I can comfortably reach with a 1-iron.

Occasionally a hole is so long you can't get home if you hit anything less than a driver off the tee. But if that's not the case, you're much better off hitting it 230 yards into the fairway than 280 yards into the trees or a bunker. After all, for a good player, what's the difference between hitting an 8-iron or a 6-iron to the green? And if you're in the fairway, you have a much better chance of playing the shot that needs to be played.

Fought, the 1977 U.S. Amateur champion, was named Golf Digest's Rookie of the Year in 1979 when he won two tournaments on the PGA Tour, the Buick-Goodwrench Open and the Anheuser-Busch Classic. The Brigham Young graduate has won $385,788 in seven years on tour.

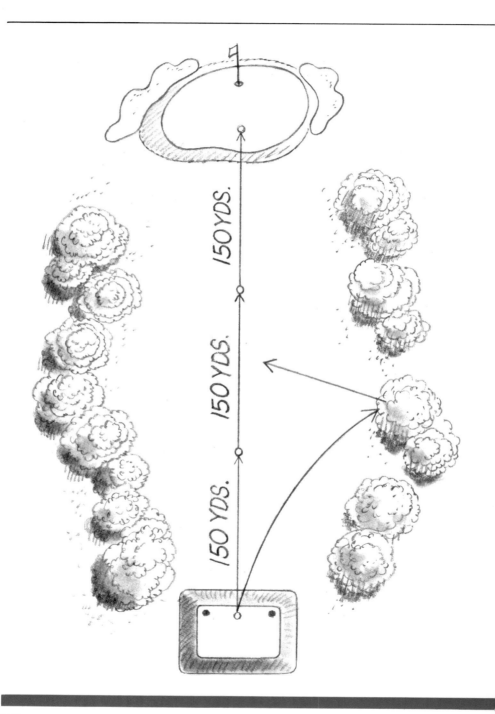

150 YDS.

150 YDS.

150 YDS.

Plan your round and club selection according to your handicap

Fought's lesson for good players has wider application, in my view. You should plan your round and club selection according to your skill level. Your handicap is a good guide to what *you* can do. If you shoot 90, you're approximately an 18-handicapper. That means your "par" is a bogey on each hole. You are allowed two putts per hole, which means you have an extra shot to reach each green. Look how easy that makes it—if you're playing a 360-yard par-4 hole, you have three shots to reach the green before using your two putts. You're only required to average 120 yards per shot! Surely, most golfers are capable of that.

Yet so many golfers don't think of club selection in those terms. You've got to do what Fought suggests and pick clubs you can *control*, then follow your plan throughout the round and don't abandon it the first time you stumble. Just taking a driver and blasting away might seem like the macho thing to do, but it's often counterproductive for the average player. A 1-iron isn't much easier, but the point is to pick clubs you can handle and keep the ball in play. Let your one-putts lower your handicap, not the wild pursuit of a little extra distance.

Keep in mind: To shoot 79 on a golf course that is 6,450 yards long, your average shot only needs to be 150 yards!

SPECIALTY

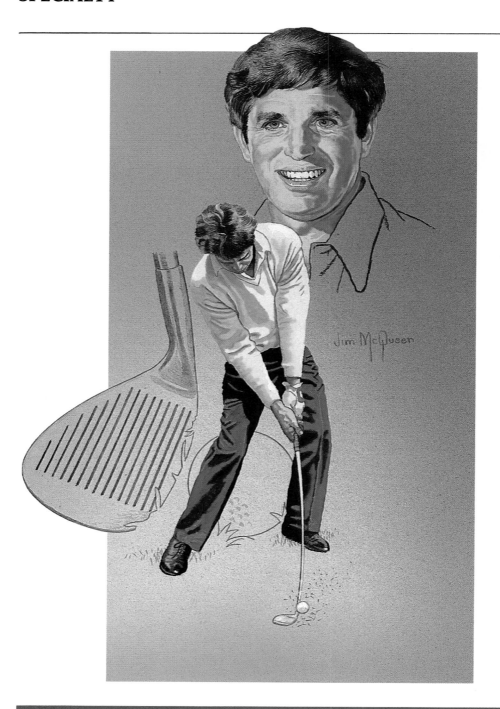

Jim McQueen

Lay a sand wedge flat to hit the ball high

By DAVE EICHELBERGER

Any time you need an extremely high shot —over a close-in bunker, a tree or a bush—you can use this method. Take a sand wedge and lay the clubface wide open, the blade pointing almost straight up in the air and the back of the club almost flat on the ground. Take a wider stance than normal, set up very open and play the ball forward. Of course you need a decent lie so you can get the club under the ball.

Then just swing hard, with no extra hand action or manipulation, although you do take the club a little outside because of your open stance. The harder you swing, the quicker the ball will get up and the higher it will fly. You have to swing hard because you've taken almost all the loft off the club and there's nothing to propel the ball forward. Everything is going up. I can make the ball literally go straight up if I want to.

I can use the shot from up to 60 yards or so, but it's also good for little shots—if you're very close to a hedge or bush, for example. I've been in that position many times and have heard people in the gallery asking what I'm going to do. They can't believe it when I pop the ball straight up over it.

Eichelberger has won four tournaments and $788,841 in 19 years on the PGA Tour, including the Greater Milwaukee Open twice (1971 and 1977). He was a member of the 1965 U.S. Walker Cup team while attending Oklahoma State University.

SPECIALTY

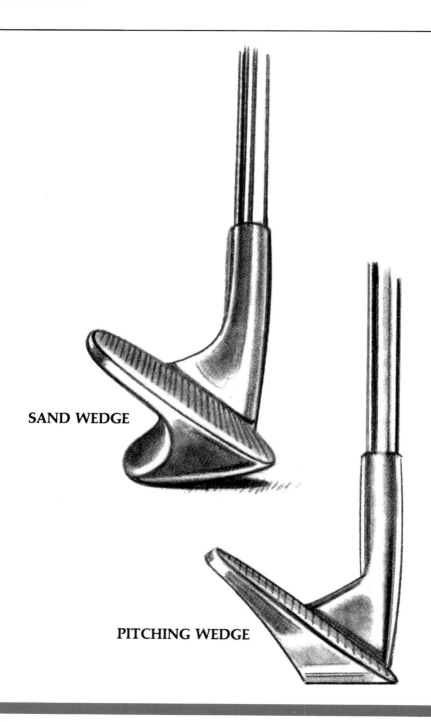

SAND WEDGE

PITCHING WEDGE

Use a sand wedge only with a good lie— otherwise, try the PW

Dave's shot is hit with the sand wedge, and good players usually have a good, well-designed sand wedge in their bags. As we discussed in previous tips, this club has a different flange than the other irons. The back of the flange is angled lower than the leading edge, and this back edge serves as a "rudder" as the club goes through the grass. The more the club is opened or laid back, the more this flange protrudes. Therefore, before you can use the sand wedge you must have enough "air" under the ball for the flange to fit. If you use a wide-flanged club, for example, you would need quite a lot of cushion under the ball before this shot is available to you.

However, you can get almost as much loft by using the pitching wedge. Because the PW doesn't have this rudder edge, it can be used from more lies than the SW.

This is a high-risk shot because of the amount of speed necessary to hit the ball any distance. Should you hit the ball thin, you'll hit a home run of epic proportions. So practice the shot to become familiar with it, experimenting with the pitching wedge, and use it when you have to.

Chip with a wood from greenside rough

By GARDNER DICKINSON

If you've watched the U.S. Open or the PGA Championship, you know the nightmare of greenside chip shots from thick rough. This rough can grab the blade of an iron and stop it cold, ruining the shot.

Here's a suggestion I got from Ken Mattiace, who played on the Tournament Players Series circuit: Chip with a wood. No kidding. Choke down on your favorite wood club. I use a driver; some of my friends prefer

Bafflers. Play the ball back in your stance, keep your hands forward and "putt" the ball the way you would if you were using a heavy mallet putter.

The idea is to sweep through the ball with the clubhead. The wood head will slide through the grass much more easily than an iron. If the ball is nestled tightly in the grass, you might want to bring the club up abruptly on the backswing and "pop" it onto the green.

A highly respected player and teacher who won seven tournaments on the PGA Tour from 1956–1971, back problems have limited Dickinson's play on the Senior PGA Tour in recent years. He teamed with Sam Snead to win the 1978 Legends of Golf. He is married to Judy Clark Dickinson, whom he helped improve from an 8-handicapper in 1977 to a leading player on the LPGA Tour.

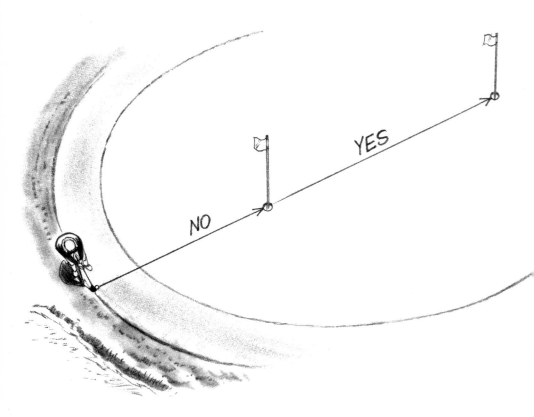

Practice to gain feel for such a shot and be sure to allow room for it to run

Gardner's tip gives us yet another great example of the imagination tour players possess. I must admit I had not heard of this one before. But after trying it myself and trying it on some club players, I had good results in certain situations. But there are a couple of things to keep in mind when you try it.

First, the loft of the driver is the least of any club, therefore you should use it only if there is lots of room for the ball to run on the green. The ball will react much like it would if you were chipping with a 1-iron from a good lie.

Secondly, the lie of a wood club is flatter than that of an iron. Therefore, you have to stand farther away from the ball which creates a flatter swing. That swing will enter the tall grass sooner on the downswing than the more upright swing of a short iron.

Finally, the feel at contact is different. So you've got to practice this type of shot quite a bit to become comfortable enough to use it in competition. But when you get the opportunity to play this shot in a match, just watch your partner's eyes when you pull that headcover off!